HOLIDAY ORIGAMI

Halloween
Origami

by Ruth Owen

PowerKiDS press™

New York

Published in 2013 by The Rosen Publishing Group, Inc.
29 East 21st Street, New York, NY 10010

Produced for Rosen by Ruby Tuesday Books Ltd
Editor for Ruby Tuesday Books Ltd: Mark J. Sachner
US Editor: Sara Antill
Designer: Emma Randall

Photo Credits:
Cover, 1, 3, 5 (background), 7 (top left), 7 (top right), 8 (bottom), 9 (top right), 12 (bottom), 13 (top right), 16 (bottom left), 19, 20 (right), 21 (top right), 25 (top right), 28 (top), 29 (top right) © Shutterstock; 7 (bottom) © Wikipedia Creative Commons, Dr. Robert Lang. Origami models © Ruby Tuesday Books Ltd.

Library of Congress Cataloging-in-Publication Data

Owen, Ruth, 1967–
 Halloween origami / by Ruth Owen.
    p. cm. — (Holiday origami)
Includes index.
 ISBN 978-1-4488-7862-8 (library binding) — ISBN 978-1-4488-7921-2 (pbk.) —
ISBN 978-1-4488-7927-4 (6-pack)
1. Origami—Juvenile literature. 2. Halloween decorations—Juvenile literature. I. Title.
TT870.O95 2013
 736'.982—dc23

                                    2012007632

Manufactured in the United States of America

CPSIA Compliance Information: Batch # B4S12PK: For Further Information contact Rosen Publishing, New York, New York at 1-800-237-9932

Contents

Origami in Action

Take a single sheet of square paper.
Fold and crease, fold and crease,
and pretty soon you will have made
a bird, a boat, a bat, or even
a jack-o'-lantern. That's **origami**!

Origami is the art of folding paper to make
small **sculptures**, or models.

Unlike stone sculptures, paper artwork
does not last for centuries. So no one
knows for sure when or where people
first began making paper sculptures.

One place where paper folding has been popular for
hundreds of years is Japan. Origami gets its name from
the Japanese words "ori," which means "folding," and "kami,"
which means "paper."

If you've never tried origami before, that's no problem.
This book will take you step-by-step through six fun Halloween
origami projects. All you need is some paper and to get folding!

Get Folding!

Before you get started on your Halloween origami models, here are some tips.

Tip 1
Read all the instructions carefully and look at the pictures. Make sure you understand what's required before you begin a fold. Don't rush, but be patient. Work slowly and carefully.

Tip 2
Folding a piece of paper sounds easy, but it can be tricky to get neat, accurate folds. The more you practice, the easier it becomes.

Tip 3
If an instruction says "crease," make the crease as flat as possible. The flatter the creases, the better the model. You can make a sharp crease by running a plastic ruler along the edge of the paper.

Tip 4
Sometimes, at first, your models may look a little crumpled. Don't give up! The more models you make, the better you will get at folding and creasing.

When it comes to origami, practice makes perfect!

Just take a look at some of these models made
by experienced origami model makers. Keep practicing
and you could become an origami master!

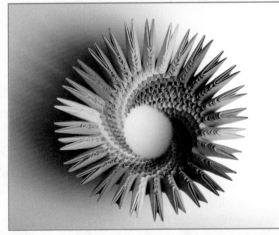

This incredible shape is made from
many models joined together.

An origami swan

Dr. Robert Lang, an origami expert, folds an American flag from a single piece of paper.

The Ghosts of Halloween

We celebrate Halloween on October 31. Around 2,000 years ago, the **Celtic** people of Ireland, Britain, and France celebrated their New Year's Eve on this date. For the Celts, October 31 marked the end of summer and the start of winter, a season of darkness.

The Celts believed that on the night of October 31, the barriers between the **spirit** world and the human world were at their weakest. This was the night when the ghosts of the dead returned to Earth to roam the countryside!

To make a ghost, you will need:

A sheet of white or gray
origami paper

A black marker

(Origami paper is sometimes colored on both sides or white on one side.)

STEP 1:
Place the paper
colored side
down. Fold
the paper
diagonally,
and crease.

STEP 2:
Fold both sides
into the center
along the dotted
lines, and crease.

Pockets

STEP 3:
Fold both sides at the bottom
into the center along the dotted
lines, and crease.
You will create two pockets at
the bottom of the model.

STEP 4:
This next
part is tricky!
Unfold one of
the bottom
pockets.
Your model
should look
like this.

Pocket

STEP 5:

Gently fold and collapse the pocket to look like this.

STEP 6:

Lift up the bottom pocket on the left side of the model. Gently fold and collapse the pocket. Check that your model looks like this.

STEP 7:

Flip the model over. Fold both sides into the center along the dotted lines, and crease.

STEP 8:

Flip the model back over and fold down points A and B.

A   B

STEP 9:
Fold the point at the top of the model down behind the model.

STEP 10:
Fold the point at the bottom of the model backward to make a tail.

STEP 11:
Fold the point of the tail again.

STEP 12:
Use the marker to give your ghost a scary or friendly face.

Origami Jack-o'-Lanterns

In ancient times, the Celts built bonfires to scare away evil spirits at Halloween.

In Ireland, people made jack-o'-lanterns to frighten away unfriendly ghosts. They carved scary faces in potatoes and turnips and put glowing coals inside. This **tradition** began with an Irish **myth** about a man named Jack who played tricks on the devil. When trickster Jack died, God would not let him into heaven, and the devil would not let him into hell. Carrying his lantern carved from a turnip, "Jack of the lantern" was doomed to walk the Earth as a ghost.

When Europeans settled in America, they used the pumpkins that grew there to make jack-o'-lanterns for Halloween.

To make origami jack-o'-lanterns, you will need:

A black marker

Sheets of orange origami paper

(Origami paper is sometimes colored on both sides or white on one side.)

STEP 2:
Fold the triangle you've made in half again, and crease

STEP 1:
Place the paper colored side down. Fold the paper diagonally, and crease.

A

A

Pocket

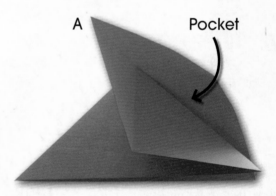

STEP 3:
Now take Corner A and fold back along the dotted line.

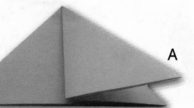

A

STEP 4:
Take hold of corner A and lift up. Then open up the pocket. Check that what you have looks like this picture.

STEP 5:
Now gently squash down the pocket so it collapses to form a square.

STEP 6:
Flip your model over so it looks like this.

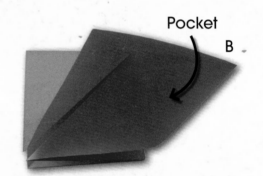

Pocket

B

STEP 7:
Now take corner B and fold it back along the dotted line. (You should now have a square shape.)

STEP 8:
Take hold of corner B, lift, and open up the pocket. Check that what you have looks like this picture.

STEP 9:
Now, gently push down on corner B and the model should collapse so that corner B meets corner C. Check your model is a square shape.

STEP 10:
Fold the two top layers of paper (D and E) into the center.

Flap E is
tucked under

D

STEP 11:
Now tuck flaps D and E
under themselves.

F   G

STEP 12:
Fold in the two top
edges F and G.

STEP 13:
Now tuck flaps
F and G under
themselves.

STEP 14:
Fold the top and bottom points
behind the model, and crease well.

STEP 15:
Fold the two sides behind the
model, and crease well.

STEP 16:
Use the marker to give
your pumpkin a gruesome
mouth and eyes!

Halloween Claws

Many hundreds of years ago, people believed that spirits roamed the Earth on the night of October 31.

If people left their homes after dark, they dressed up so the ghosts would think they were fellow spirits and not know they were human. People disguised themselves by wearing masks or putting ash from the fire on their faces.

Today, we still dress up for Halloween. On the night of the 31st, the streets are filled with ghosts, werewolves, witches, zombies, and vampires!

To make claws for your Halloween costume, you will need:

One sheet of origami paper for each claw

(Origami paper is sometimes colored on both sides or white on one side.)

STEP 2:
Fold both sides into the center along the dotted lines, and crease.

STEP 1:
Place the paper colored side down. Fold the paper diagonally, and crease.

STEP 3:
Fold the model in half along the center, and crease.

STEP 4:
Fold the model along the dotted line.

STEP 5:
Now fold point A behind the model. Wrap the paper tightly because you are now forming the pointy finger.

A

A

STEP 6:
Your model should look like this.

STEP 7:
Fold point A across the model. Then tuck point A into the pocket.

Section B

STEP 8:
Slide your finger inside the model at section B and gently pop the claw open.
Your claw is ready to wear!

Point A tucks into here

STEP 9:

Make a claw for each of your fingers and thumbs. Choose a paper color that works well with your costume. Green paper is great for spiky witchlike fingers.

It's Witchcraft!

What is old, ugly, has warts and a hooked nose, wears a pointy black hat, and flies around on a broomstick? It's a witch!

In folklore (old beliefs) and in fairy tales and other children's stories, a witch is a woman who uses her magical powers to cast spells. In fairy tales, witches are often the "bad guys" who use witchcraft to harm people. In some stories, such as "Hansel and Gretel" and *The Wizard of Oz,* they are especially harmful to children!

Witches are a popular costume choice at Halloween!

To make a spooky witch, you will need:

Two sheets of black
origami paper

Colored pens

(Origami paper is sometimes colored on both sides or white on one side.)

STEP 1:
Place the paper
colored side
down. Fold the
paper diagonally,
and crease.

STEP 2:
Fold both
sides into the
center along
the dotted
lines, and
crease.

STEP 3:
Fold the bottom half
of the model up along
the dotted line,
and crease.

STEP 4:
Now fold the top layer of
paper back down toward
you along the dotted
line, and crease.

STEP 5:
Your model should now look like this.

STEP 6:
Flip your model over. Fold in on the two dotted lines, and crease. These are tricky folds to make!

STEP 7:
The back of your model should look like this.

STEP 8:
This next part is tricky. Gently pull the little pockets at A and B outward and flatten.

A   B

STEP 9:
The back of your model should now look like this.

STEP 10:
Flip the model over. Draw a face on your witch.

STEP 11:
To make the witch's body, repeat steps 1 and 2 with a new sheet of paper.

STEP 12:
Fold up the bottom point and crease.

STEP 13:
Fold down the top point so that it overlaps the bottom point.

STEP 14:
Now make two folds along the dotted lines.

Back view

Front view

STEP 15:
Tuck the top of the body under the back of the witch's hat. Unfold parts C and D, and your witch should be able to stand.

C   D

Witch's Cat

Why are witches often shown with a black cat?

In folklore and in fairy tales, witches sometimes have a special companion that helps them perform their magic. This helper is known as a "familiar spirit."

A witch's familiar spirit is usually an animal. The most common witch's familiar spirit is a black cat. Some witches, however, have a toad, an owl, or a dog as a familiar spirit.

24

To make the witch's cat, you will need:

Two sheets of black origami paper

Glue

 Green beads or fake gemstones

A black marker

(Origami paper is sometimes colored on both sides or white on one side.)

STEP 1:
Place the paper colored side down. Fold the paper on both diagonals, and crease.

STEP 2:
Fold the top corner down to the middle, and crease.

STEP 3:
Flip your model over. Fold up the bottom corner, and crease.

STEP 4:
Flip your model over again.

25

STEP 5:
Fold the top half of the model over along the central crease line you made earlier.

STEP 6:
Now fold one side into the center so that its edge meets the center crease line.

STEP 7:
Fold the other half into the center. Your model should look like this.

STEP 8:
Now fold the two flaps up along the dotted lines. You are making the cat's ears.

STEP 9:
Fold down the top point to make the top of the cat's head.

STEP 10:
Flip your model over. Turn down the bottom flap to make the cat's nose.

STEP 11:
Now draw your cat a mouth and glue on gemstone eyes.

STEP 12:
To make the cat's body, place another sheet of paper colored side down. Make a diagonal fold, and crease.

STEP 13:
Fold both sides into the center along the dotted lines, and crease.

STEP 14:
Fold the model in half along the center crease.

STEP 16:
Fit the neck into the back of the cat's head, and the witch's cat is complete.

Neck

Tail

Chest

STEP 15:
Fold the thin point upward to make the cat's tail. Fold the other end in to make the cat's chest and neck.

Halloween Bats

Vampire bat

No one knows exactly why bats have become a symbol of Halloween.

Maybe it's because they flutter around at night. These gentle, flying **mammals** don't attack people, though. They are just hunting flying insects.

Maybe it's the vampire bat that makes us think of horror movies and spooky things. This type of bat lives in parts of Mexico, Central America, and South America. Vampire bats feed by sinking their fangs into the bodies of other animals. Then they lick up the blood!

To make some bats, you will need:

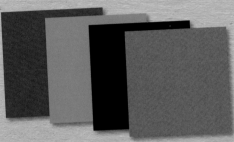

Sheets of black, gray, deep purple, and deep blue origami paper

Peel and stick goggly eyes

Scissors

(Origami paper is sometimes colored on both sides or white on one side.)

STEP 1:
Place the paper colored side down. Fold the paper in half diagonally, and crease.

STEP 2:
Unfold the paper and fold in half diagonally the other way, and crease

STEP 3:
Fold the long side of the triangle over toward you, and crease.

STEP 4:
Now you'll begin to make the bat's wings. Fold one side in along the dotted line.

STEP 5:
Check that what you have looks like this picture.

Top of model   Top of wing

STEP 6:
Now fold the wing back. The top edge of the wing should be parallel to the top of the model.

STEP 7:
To make the other wing, fold in along the dotted line.

STEP 8:
Now fold the wing back. Keep the top edge of the wing parallel to the top of the model.

Ear   Ear

STEP 9:
Now, to make the bat's ears, use the scissors to cut along the dotted line on the bat's head.

STEP 10:
You can add eyes to your bat if you wish. Peel-and-stick goggly eyes can be bought from craft stores or from online craft suppliers.

STEP 11:
Try making a colony of bats in different colors! You can attach them to string or ribbon to make Halloween decorations.

Glossary

Celtic (KEL-tik) Related to or having to do with the religions, languages, and cultures of people and tribes who lived in parts of modern-day Europe.

mammals (MA-mulz) Animals that generally give birth to live young, are warm-blooded, have fur or hair, and feed their young with milk from the mother.

myth (MITH) A story told to explain something in nature or society, usually including supernatural beings or events.

origami (or-uh-GAH-mee) The art of folding paper into decorative shapes or objects.

sculptures (SKULP-cherz) Works of art that have a shape to them, such as statues or carved objects, and may be made of wood, stone, metal, plaster or even paper.

spirit (SPIR-ut) Having to do with a world or realm that is not physical and may be represented by ghosts and other supernatural forms.

tradition (truh-DIH-shun) A custom, belief, or practice that has existed for a long time and has been passed on from one generation to the next.

Index

Websites

Due to the changing nature of Internet links, PowerKids Press has developed an online list of websites related to the subject of this book. This site is updated regularly. Please use this link to access the list:
www.powerkidslinks.com/horig/hallo/